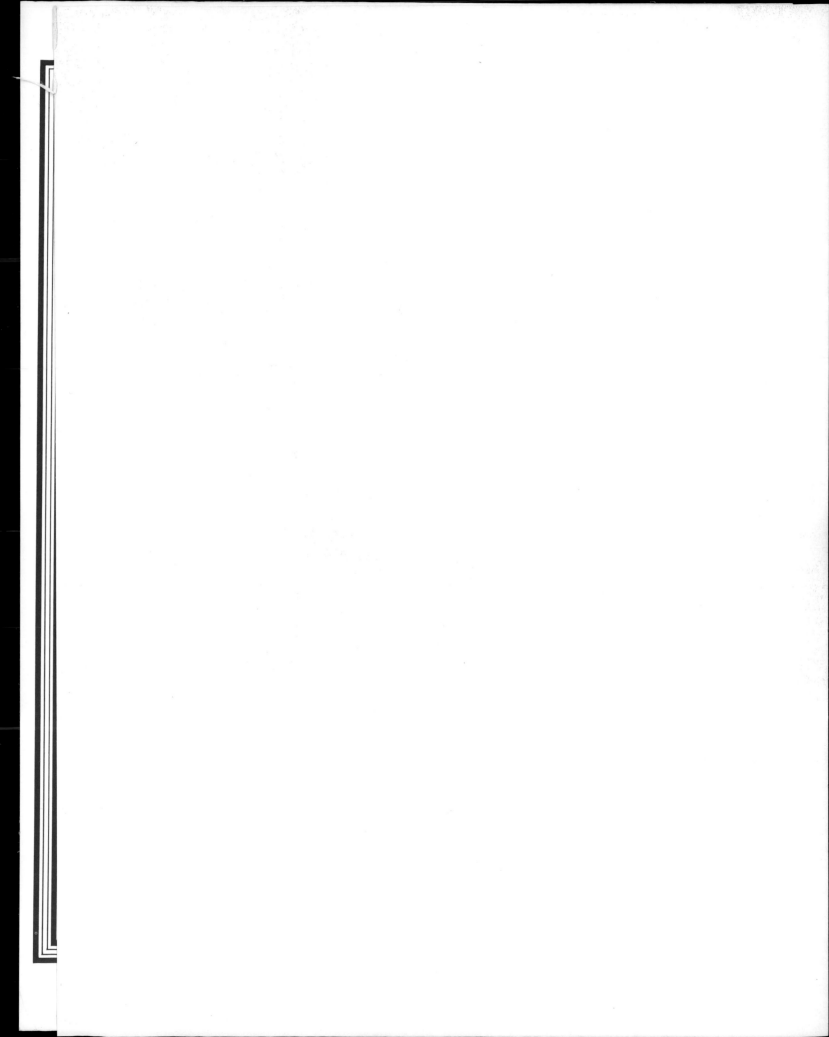

Despite his persistence, Florey had a miserable time trying to keep all the members of the team in frame. Accustomed to the stage, they ran all over the place paying little heed to the fact that the early sound cameras were immobile. The camera and the cameraman were locked inside a soundproof box to prevent the camera's clanking noise from being picked up by the sound equipment. In addition, the camera could not be panned very much. To do so would result in a beautiful picture of the inside of the box. Florey finally resolved his problem by seeing to it that several cameras were kept going. If one Marx Brother jumped out of frame, Florey would have enough close-ups to cover the action until the delinquent could be gestured back in scene.

In later interviews, Groucho repeatedly faults Florey for not being able to speak English very well—Florey is a Frenchman. But the accusations seem unfounded. The director was able to do a truly cinematic job of filming. THE COCOANUTS may be the very first Broadway musical film. He even pre-dated Busby Berkeley with some extraordinary visuals in dance sequences such as The Monkey Doodle-Doo routine which finds Florey's camera switching to various high and low angles. He accomplished this by shooting parts of the sequence silent. This enabled him to use a lighter camera which he was able to hoist to the top of the stage and move in on various aspects of the choreographed piece. The resulting film was a tremendous hit and the only sad part of the whole thing was that the Marx Bros. couldn't attend the gala Broadway opening of the film at the Rialto Theater. They were two blocks away performing ANIMAL CRACKERS at the Forty-Fourth Street Theater.

Soon after the opening of THE COCOANUTS movie, the Marxes traipsed back to the Astoria Studios and recorded ANIMAL CRACKERS . "Record" is the best word to describe the result. Probably due to Groucho's displeasure, Florey was not directing the new film. Only after screening THE COCOANUTS back to back with ANIMAL CRACKERS can you become fully aware of Florey's contributions. The new director was Victor Heerman who did nothing more than set his camera up and record the musical, scene by scene. A total lack of filmmaking sense is displayed, even in the cutting room. The final film has a number of mis-matched scenes. Coupled with an abominable soundtrack and poor photography, the film is misleading as to the quality of sound films possible in 1930.

Yet, these first two Marx Bros. movies remain today, in my mind, the most important record we have of the team. Certainly they are not their best films, for it wasn't until the team went over to Metro-Goldwyn-Mayer, under the guidance of Irving Thalberg, that they were to work in a disciplined fashion to produce the crème de la crème of their long career, A NIGHT AT THE OPERA and A DAY AT THE RACES.

Recall that Woollcott/Kaufman story. Here is the clue to the importance of those first two Paramount features. As the team became more and more entrenched in Hollywood—they moved there right after the filming of ANIMAL CRACKERS—they relied upon more and more writers for their material. Sure, everything was written in the style of the Marx Bros., certainly with their approval, but still the writers' personalities came through. Is S.J. Perelman so anonymous in MONKEY BUSINESS and HORSE-FEATHERS? Hardly, with lines such as, "That's what they said to Thomas Edison, mighty inventor; Thomas Lindbergh, mighty flier and Thomas Shefsky, mighty lak a rose." Only a wit intimately aware of New York's Yiddish Theater could have composed such a line.

But THE COCOANUTS and ANIMAL CRACKERS are different. Each was performed on the New York stage and around the country over a thousand times. As the shows progressed and the Marxes were left to their own devices, they began to improvise. More and more of the Kaufman/Ryskind lines began to disappear as pure Marx humor, vaudeville humor emerged once again. The most drastic changes seem to have occurred in ANIMAL CRACKERS which was in the middle of its run when the stock market crash sent fortunes tumbling and suddenly penniless socialites flying out of windows. The night of the crash saw several references to it in ANIMAL CRACKERS . The Marxes—all except Chico who never kept any money to lose—were hard hit by the crash and there could be no way they wouldn't comment on it. The film is loaded with remarks on the financial ruin, especially in Spaulding's conversation with Chandler.

My point here is that it may very well be that the only records we have of pure Marx humor are the first two Paramount films. True, Morrie Ryskind worked on the scripts for the films, but certainly the tried and true adlibs were retained for the filmization of each show. This is the historical importance of these films, coupled with the fact that each of them offer a marvelous opportunity for us to get a good impression of what a Broadway musical looked like in the twenties and thirties.

Until recently, ANIMAL CRACKERS could not be seen in the United States. Universal Pictures now owns the film, but for the last two decades the literary rights were in the hands of the George S. Kaufman Estate. Thus, Universal had the picture with no words and the Estate had the words with no picture. Neither could move without the other and peculiarities inherent in lawyers' thinking kept it that way.

But now the film is available and this book is possible. Because of the legal stalemate, ANIMAL CRACKERS had to be excluded from *Why a Duck?*, my first book on the Marx Bros. This volume is meant to correct that situation.

Over 800 frame blow-ups coupled with the original dialogue bring you some of the funniest moments from ANIMAL CRACKERS in book form. With the exception of their last few films, noticeably devoid of funny material, I have been able to bring together what I consider to be the funniest excerpts of the film career of the Marx Bros. in two volumes. In between, I had the distinct pleasure of working with Groucho on *The Marx Bros. Scrapbook*. Despite my falling out with Groucho over that book, I am pleased that I had the opportunity to successfully develop that project and collect some fifty hours of interviews with him, his brothers Gummo and Zeppo and a host of other personalities involved with the career of the team.

My work on all these books has given me an invaluable education in the formative years of American entertainment, especially the motion picture industry in which I am intensely interested. It is my hope that these three volumes combined will form a lasting record of the life and times of the Marx Bros.

Richard J. Anobile
New York City
August, 1974

Acknowledgments

I take this opportunity to thank those individuals and organizations whose cooperation has made this book possible.

The right to produce this book was granted to us by Universal Pictures, Inc., and by the George S. Kaufman Estate and by Mr. Morrie Ryskind. I would especially like to thank Mr. Steve Adler and Mr. Stanley Newman of Universal, Mr. David Grossberg of the firm of Cohen and Grossberg, as well as Mrs. Anne Kaufman Schneider and Mr. Ryskind.

Mr. Harold Goldberg of Universal's New York office was very helpful in seeing to it that all materials needed were made available to me.

Alyne Model and George Norris of Riverside Film Associates once again handled all the technical aspects of this project. They accurately transferred my frame selections to the negative and saw to it that the frames I picked were the ones I received. All blow-ups were produced by Vita Print in New York under the watchful eye of Saul Jaffe. For help with typing and administrative details, I am grateful to Ms. Vivien Rowan and Ms. Valerie Beale.

Harry Chester Associates was responsible for the design of the book and once again used great skill and imagination in making the film come to life on the printed page.

—Richard J. Anobile

Based on the Musical Play
by

GEORGE S. KAUFMAN   MORRIE RYSKIND
BERT KALMAR   HARRY RUBY

Screen Play By   *Continuity By*
MORRIE RYSKIND   PIERRE COLLINGS

Photographed By
GEORGE FOLSEY

PASSED BY THE NATIONAL BOARD OF REVIEW

THE PLAYERS

Captain Jeffrey Spaulding	GROUCHO MARX
The Professor	HARPO MARX
Signor Emanuel Ravelli	CHICO MARX
Horatio Jamison	ZEPPO MARX
Arabella Rittenhouse	LILLIAN ROTH
Mrs. Rittenhouse	MARGARET DUMONT
Roscoe Chandler	LOUIS SORIN
John Parker	HAL THOMPSON
Mrs. Whitehead	MARGARET IRVING
Grace Carpenter	KATHRYN REECE
Hives	ROBERT GREIG
Hennessey	EDWARD METCALF
Six Footmen	The MUSIC MASTERS

SOCIAL SEASON OPENS WITH BRILLIANT HOUSE PARTY AT HOME OF MRS. RITTENHOUSE

Captain Geoffrey T. Spaulding, Noted Explorer Returning from Africa, to be Guest of Honor

Roscoe W. Chandler Wealthy Art Patron will Exhibit Beaugard's Famous Painting "AFTER THE HUNT" at

THE RITTENHOUSE HOME

One of the showplaces of Long Island

Chandler: Mrs. Rittenhouse, Captain Spaulding has arrived.

Mrs. Rittenhouse: Oh, I'm so glad. My friends, Captain Spaulding has arrived.

Guests: *At last we are to meet him, The famous Captain Spaulding, From climates hot and scalding, The Captain has arrived.*

Guests: *Most heartily we'll greet him, With plain and fancy cheering, Until he's hard of hearing, The Captain has arrived.*

Guests: *At last the Captain has arrived.*
Hives: Mr. Horatio W. Jamison, Field Secretary to Captain Spaulding.

Jamison: *I represent the Captain who insists on my informing you of these conditions under which he camps here.*

Jamison: *In one thing he is very strict. He wants his women young and picked.*

Jamison: *And as for men, he won't have any tramps here.*

Crowd: *And as for men, he won't have any tramps here. There must be no tramps,*

Jamison: *The men must all be very old, The women warm, The champagne cold.*

Jamison: *It's under these conditions that he camps here.*

Hives: I'm announcing Captain Jeffrey Spaulding!

Guests: *Oh, dear, he is coming.*

Guests: *He's announcing Captain Jeffrey Spaulding.*

Guests: *At last he is here.*

Spaulding: Well, what do I owe you?

Native: Samla, Samlakita, Samlasha!

Spaulding: What? From Africa to here, $1.85? That's an outrage. I told you not to take me through Australia. You know it's all ripped up.

Spaulding: You should have come right up Lincoln Boulevard.

Spaulding: Turn around the rear end. I want to see your license plates. I don't...

Mrs. Rittenhouse: Captain Spaulding...

Spaulding: I'll attend to you later. **Mrs. Rittenhouse:** Captain Spaulding...

Mrs. Rittenhouse: Captain Spaulding, Rittenhouse Manor is entirely at your disposal.

Spaulding: Well, you're one of the most beautiful women I've ever seen and that's not saying much for you.

Spaulding: Well, I certainly am grateful for this magnificent wash-out . . . I mean turn-out.

Spaulding: And now, I'd like to say a few words.

Spaulding: *Hello—I must be going,*
I cannot stay,
I came to say,
I must be going.

Spaulding: *I'm glad I came,*
But just the same,
I must be going.

Spaulding: *Tra, la!*

Mrs. Rittenhouse: *For my sake you must stay,*

Mrs. Rittenhouse: *If you should go away,*
You'd spoil this party I am throwing.

Spaulding: *I'll stay a week or two,*

Spaulding: *I'll stay the summer through,*
But I am telling you
I must be going.

Guests: *Before you go,*
Will you oblige us,
And tell us of
Your deeds so glowing?

Spaulding: *I'll do anything you say,*
In fact, I'll even stay.
Guests: *Good!*

Spaulding: *But, I must be going!*

Jamison: *There's something that I'd like to state,*

Jamison: *That he's too modest to relate, The Captain is a very moral man, Sometimes he finds it trying.*

Spaulding: *This fact I'll emphasize with stress,*
I never take a drink, unless . . .

Spaulding: *Somebody's buying.*

Guests: *The Captain is a very moral man!*

Jamison: *If he hears anything obscene,*
He'll naturally repel it.

Spaulding: *I hate a dirty joke, I do,*
Unless it's told by someone, who . . .

Spaulding: *Knows how to tell it.*

Guests: *The Captain is a very moral man.*

Guests: *Hooray for Captain Spaulding.*

Guests: *The African Explorer!*

Spaulding: *Did someone call me, "Schnorrer?"*

Guests: *Hooray!*

Guests: *Hooray! Hooray!*

Jamison: *He went into the jungle, Where all the monkeys throw nuts.*

Spaulding: *If I stay here, I'll go nuts.*

Guests: *Hooray! Hooray! Hooray!*

Guests: *He put all his reliance.*

Guests: *In courage and defiance*
And risked his life for science.

Spaulding: *Hey! Hey!*

Mrs. Rittenhouse: *He is the only white man, Who covered every acre.*

Spaulding: *I think I'll try and make her.*

Guests: *Hooray! Hooray! Hooray!*

33

Guests: *He put all his reliance, In courage and defiance. And risked his life for science.*

Spaulding: *Hey! Hey!*
Guests: *Hooray for Captain Spaulding, The African Explorer,*

Guests: *He brought his name undying fame And that is why we say, Hooray! Hooray! Hooray!*

Spaulding: My friends, I am highly gratified at this magnificent display of effusion, and I want you to know...
Guests: *Hooray for Captain Spaulding,*

Guests: *The African Explorer,*
He brought his name undying fame
And that is why we say,

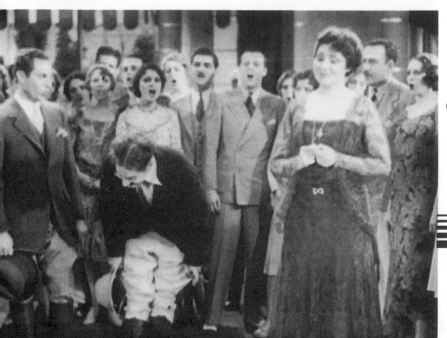

Guests: *Hooray!*

Guests:
Hooray! Hooray!

Spaulding: My friends,
I am highly gratified at this
magnificent display of
effusion and I want you
to know . . .
Guests: *Hooray for
Captain Spaulding,*

Guests: *The African
Explorer, He brought his
name undying fame
And that is why we say,*

Guests: *Hooray! Hooray! Hooray!*

Spaulding: My friends, I am highly gratified at this magnificent display of effusion and I want you to know...

Spaulding: *Hooray for Captain Spaulding, The African Explorer...*

Spaulding: Well, somebody's got to do it.

Mrs. Rittenhouse: Captain Spaulding, it is indeed a great honor to welcome you to my poor home...

Spaulding: Oh, it isn't so bad...
Mrs. Rittenhouse: Needless to say I...
Spaulding: Wait a minute...I think you're right. It is pretty bad.

Spaulding: As a matter of fact, it's one of the frowsiest looking joints I've ever seen.
Mrs. Rittenhouse: Why Captain!

Spaulding: Where did you get your wall paper?
Mrs. Rittenhouse: Why I . . .
Spaulding: You're letting this place run down and what's the result? You're not getting the class of people that you used to.

Spaulding: Why you've got people here now that look like you.

Spaulding: Now I'll tell you what we'll do. We'll put up a sign outside: *"Place under new management."* We'll set up a seventy-five cent meal that'll knock their *eyes* out.

Spaulding: And after we knock their *eyes* out, we can charge them anything *we* want.

Spaulding: Now sign here and give me your check for $1500.

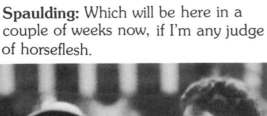

Spaulding: Which will be here in a couple of weeks now, if I'm any judge of horseflesh.

Spaulding: Now I want to tell you madam that with this insurance policy you have provided for your little ones and for your old age,

Spaulding: And now, Madam, the time has come, the walrus said . . .
Mrs. Rittenhouse: Captain Spaulding!
Spaulding: To speak of . . .

Mrs. Rittenhouse: Captain Spaulding, you stand before me as one of the bravest men of all times . . .

Spaulding: All right, I'll do that.

Mrs. Rittenhouse: In the dark forests of Africa, there has been no danger that you haven't dared.

Spaulding: Do you mind if I don't smoke?

Mrs. Rittenhouse: Fearlessly you have blazed new trails, scornful of the lion's roar, and the cannibal's tom-tom.

Spaulding: Says you!

Mrs. Rittenhouse: Never once in all those weary months did your footsteps falter. Cowardice is unknown to you. Fear is not in you.

Chandler: Pardon me,

Chandler: a caterpillar.

Spaulding: Ahh!

Mrs. Rittenhouse: Oh, Captain!

Mrs. Rittenhouse: Put him here.

Mrs. Rittenhouse: It must have been the caterpillar that frightened him.

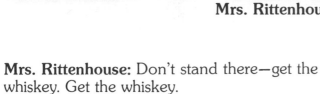

Mrs. Rittenhouse: Don't stand there—get the whiskey. Get the whiskey.
Chandler: The whiskey . . . the whiskey . . . where is the whiskey?

Spaulding: It's in my little black bag. In the right hand corner.

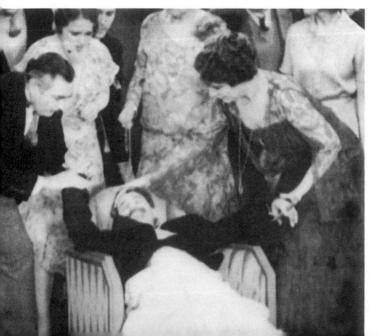

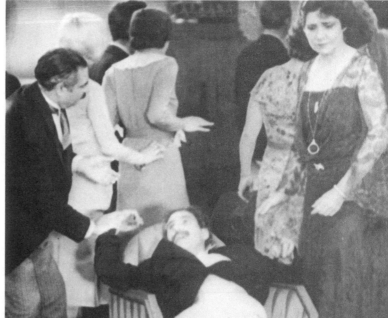

Hives: Signor Emanuel Ravelli!

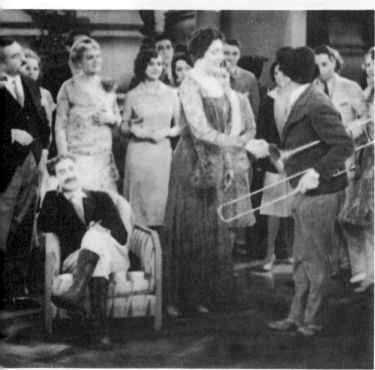

Ravelli: How do you do?
Mrs. Rittenhouse: How do you do?
Ravelli: Where is the dining room?
Mrs. Rittenhouse: I'm surprised.

Spaulding: Say, I used to
know a fellow that
looked exactly like you
by the name of Emanuel Ravelli.

Spaulding: Are you
his brother?

Ravelli: I'm Emanuel
Ravelli.
Spaulding: You're
Emanuel Ravelli?
Ravelli: I'm Emanuel
Ravelli.

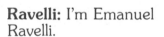

Spaulding: Well, no wonder
you look like him. But I still insist
there is a resemblance.

Ravelli: Ha, ha! He thinks I look alike.

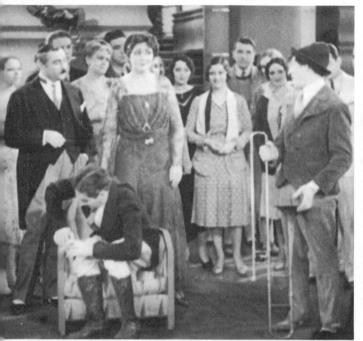

Spaulding: Well, if you do it's a tough break for both of you.

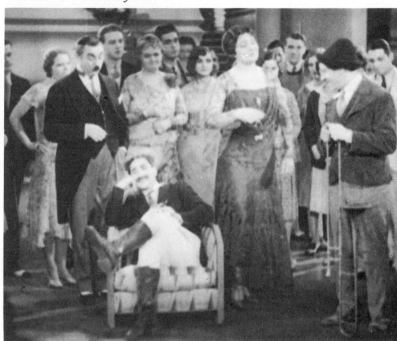

Mrs. Rittenhouse: You are one of the musicians? But you were not due until tomorrow.

Ravelli: Couldn't come tomorrow. That's too quick.

Spaulding: Say, you're lucky they didn't come yesterday.

Ravelli: We were busy yesterday, but we charge just the same.
Spaulding: This is better than exploring.

Spaulding: What do you fellows get an hour?

Ravelli: Ah, for playing we getta ten dollars an hour.
Spaulding: I see. What do you get for not playing?
Ravelli: Twelve dollars an hour.

Spaulding: Well, clip me off a
piece of that.

Ravelli: Now... for rehearsing,
we make a special rate, that'sa
fifteen dollars an hour.
Spaulding: That's for rehearsing.

Ravelli: That'sa for rehearsing.
Spaulding: And what do you get
for not rehearsing?

Ravelli: You couldn't afford it.

Ravelli: You see if we don't rehearse we don't play. And if we don't play that runs into money.
Spaulding: How much would you want to run into an open manhole?

Ravelli: Just the cover charge.

Ravelli: Ha, ha!

Spaulding: Well, drop in, sometime.
Ravelli: Sewer!

Spaulding: Well, we cleaned that up pretty well.

Ravelli: Well, let's see how we stand...
Spaulding: Flatfooted.

Ravelli: Yesterday we didn't come. You remember yesterday we didn't come.
Spaulding: Oh, I remember!

Ravelli: That's three hundred dollars.

Spaulding: Yesterday you didn't come, that's three hundred dollars.
Ravelli: Yes, three hundred dollars.
Spaulding: Well, that's reasonable. I can see that, alright.

Ravelli: Now today we did come, that's...
Spaulding: That's a hundred you owe us.

Ravelli: Hey, I bet I'm gonna lose on the deal.

Ravelli: Tomorrow we leave ... that's worth about ...
Spaulding: A million dollars ...

Ravelli: Yeah, that's all right for me, but I got a partner.

Spaulding: What!
Mrs. Rittenhouse: A partner?

Hives: The Professor!

Spaulding: The gate swung open and
a fig newton entered.

Mrs. Rittenhouse: How do you do? *(HONK)*

Mrs. Rittenhouse: Goodness!

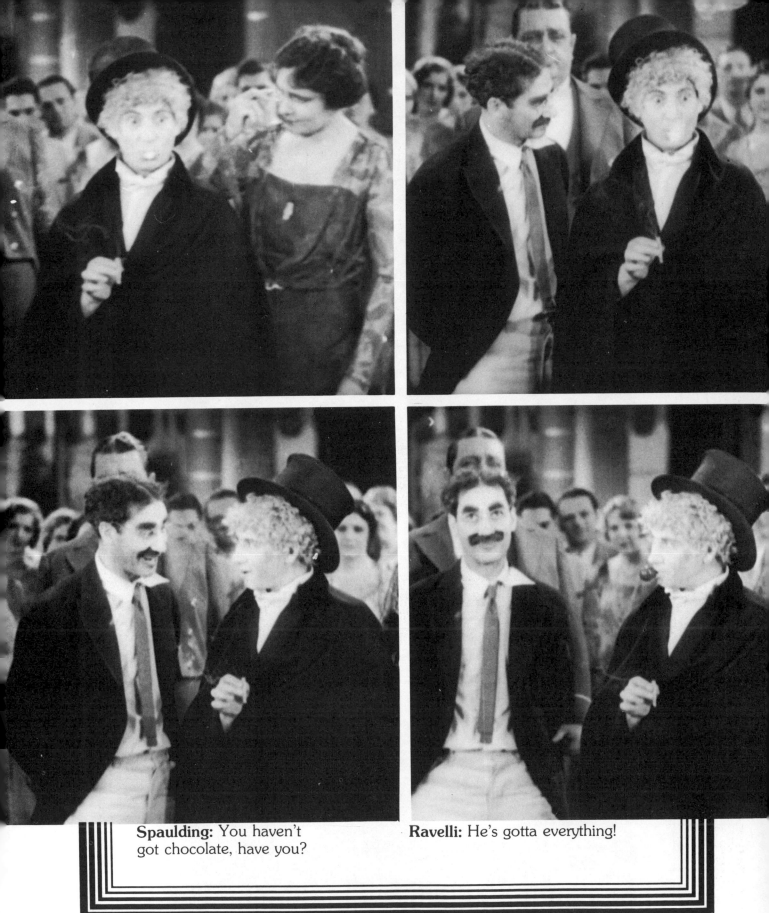

Spaulding: You haven't got chocolate, have you?

Ravelli: He's gotta everything!

Mrs. Rittenhouse: Take the Professor's hat and coat...

Spaulding: And send for the fumigators.

Chandler: What do you think this is?

Spaulding: Bonjour! Mon dieu! J'ai mal au dent.

The eternal lovers in a typical verbal joust.

Spaulding: Mrs. Rittenhouse!

Spaulding: Yoo-hoo!

Mrs. Rittenhouse:
Oh, Captain Spaulding,
how are you?

Spaulding: Tell me, are you alone?

Mrs. Rittenhouse: Why Captain,
I don't understand.

Spaulding: What, you don't
understand being alone?

Spaulding: Don't give me that
innocent stuff or you will be alone.

Spaulding: A big cluck
like you turning cute on me.

Spaulding:
Mrs. Rittenhouse . . .
Mrs. Rittenhouse:
Yes!

Spaulding:
Oh, pardon me.

Spaulding: You've been affected like this yourself at times.

Mrs. Rittenhouse: No, Captain.

Spaulding: Well, you will be.

Spaulding: Mrs. Rittenhouse, ever since I met you I've swept you off my feet.

Spaulding: Something has been throbbing within me.

Spaulding: Oh, it's been beating like the incessant tom-tom in the primitive jungle.

Spaulding: There's something that I must ask you.

Mrs. Rittenhouse: What is it, Captain?

Spaulding: Would you wash out a pair of socks for me?
Mrs. Rittenhouse: Why, Captain, I'm surprised.

Spaulding: Well, it may be a surprise to you but it's been on my mind for weeks.

Spaulding: It's just my way of telling you that I love you, that's all.

Spaulding: I love you.

Spaulding: I love you . . . There's never been . . .
Mrs. Rittenhouse: Captain!

Mrs. Whitehead: I beg your pardon, am I intruding?

Spaulding: Are you intruding? Just when I had her on the five yard line.

Spaulding: I should say you are intruding!

Spaulding: I should say you **are** intruding. Pardon me, I was using the subjunctive instead of the past tense.

Spaulding: Yes, we're away past tents. We're living in bungalows now.

Spaulding: This is a mechanical age of course.

Mrs. Rittenhouse: Mrs. Whitehead, you haven't met Captain Spaulding, have you?
Mrs. Whitehead: Why no, I haven't.

Mrs. Whitehead: How are you?
Spaulding: How are you?

Mrs. Whitehead: I'm fine, thank you. And how are you?
Spaulding: And how are you?

Spaulding: That leaves you one up.

Spaulding: Did anyone ever tell you you had beautiful eyes?
Mrs. Whitehead: No.
Spaulding: Well, you have.

Spaulding: And so have you.

Spaulding: He shot her a glance

Spaulding: as a smile played around his lips.

Spaulding: In fact I don't think I have seen four more beautiful eyes in my life. Well, three anyway.

Spaulding: You know you two girls have everything... You're tall and short, slim and stout, and blonde and brunette and that's just the kind of a girl I c-r-a-v-e. We three would make an ideal couple.

Spaulding: You've got beauty, charm, money...

Spaulding: You have got money, haven't you? Because if you haven't we can quit right now.
Mrs. Whitehead: The Captain is charming, isn't he?

Mrs. Rittenhouse: I'm fascinated.
Spaulding: I'm fascinated, too, right on the arm.

Spaulding: Fascinated! Whim! Wham!

Spaulding: If I were Eugene O'Neill I could tell you what I really think of you two.

Spaulding: You know, you're very fortunate that the Theatre Guild isn't putting this on. And so is the Guild.

Spaulding: Pardon me, while I have a Strange Interlude.

Spaulding: Well, what do you say, girls, what do you say? Will you marry me?

Mrs. Rittenhouse: But Captain, which one of us?

Spaulding: Both of you. Let's all get married. This is my party.

Spaulding: Party, party!

Here I am talking of parties. I came down here for a party. What happens? Nothing. Not even ice cream. The gods look down and laugh. This would be a better world for children if the parents had to eat spinach.

Spaulding: Well, what do you say, girls, what do you say? Are we all going to get married?
Mrs. Whitehead: All of us?
Spaulding: All of us.

Mrs. Whitehead: But that's bigamy.
Spaulding: Yes, and it's big o' me too.

Spaulding: It's big of all of us. Let's be big for a change.

Spaulding: I'm sick of these conventional marriages. One woman and one man was good enough for your grandmother, but who wants to marry your grandmother?

Spaulding: Nobody, not even your grandfather.

Spaulding: Think, think of the honeymoon, strictly private. I wouldn't let another woman in on this.

Spaulding: Well, maybe one or two.

Spaulding: But no men.

Spaulding: I may not go myself.

Mrs. Rittenhouse: Are you suggesting companionate marriage?

Spaulding: Well, it's got its advantages. You could live with your folks and I could live with your folks.

Spaulding: And you, you could sell Fuller brushes.

Spaulding: Living with your folks.

Spaulding: Well, let's see, where **were** we?

Spaulding: Oh, yes, we were about to get married. Do you think we really ought to get married?
Mrs. Rittenhouse: I think marriage is a very noble institution.

Spaulding: Ha, ha, ha, ha!

Mrs. Whitehead: It's the foundation of the American home.
Spaulding: Yes, but the trouble is you can't enforce it.

Spaulding: It was put over on the American people while our boys were over there.

Spaulding: And while our girls were over here.

Spaulding: You know, I've been waiting at the bottom of these stairs for years for just such a moment as this.

Mrs. Rittenhouse: But, Captain, where are you going?

Spaulding: I'm sorry, ladies, I'm sorry, but we'll have to postpone the wedding for a few days, maybe for a few years. Before I get married, I'm going to sow a couple of wild oats.

After a confrontation with Ravelli and The Professor, Roscoe W. Chandler, who has been robbed of more than his dignity, comes across Spaulding whose only concern is Chandler's money.

Spaulding: Hey...hey...where's your tie?

Chandler: Of course I have garters. Here!

Chandler: Oh...I...
Spaulding: That's a fine way for a millionaire to be running around, open at the neck. Have you got garters

Chandler: Oh, they've taken my garters, too!

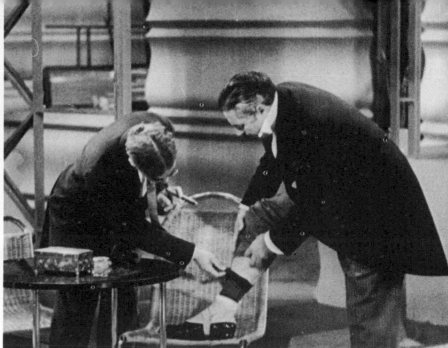

Spaulding: A likely story. Turning collegiate on me, eh? Have you got socks?
Chandler: Certainly.

Spaulding: You *have* got socks. They look pretty old to me. Whose are they?

Spaulding: Well, old socks, let me introduce myself. My name is Spaulding, Captain Spaulding.
Chandler: And I am Roscoe W. Chandler.

Spaulding: Oh, Roscoe W. Chandler! Well, this is a treat, your treat.

Chandler: You've heard about me?
Spaulding: Yes, I've heard about you for a great many of years, Mr. Chandler, and I'm gettin' pretty darn sick of it, too.

Spaulding: Well, that's fine. I've heard of you and you've heard of me.

Spaulding: Now have you heard the one about the two Irishmen?

Chandler: Oh, yes. Ha, ha, ha!

Spaulding: Well, now that I've got you in hysterics, let's get down to business. My name's Spaulding, Captain Spaulding.

Chandler: I'm Roscoe W. Chandler.
Spaulding: And I am Jeffrey T. Spaulding. I'll bet you don't know what the T. stands for?

Chandler: Ah—Thomas?

Spaulding: Edgar.

Spaulding: You were close, though. You were close though, and you still are, I'll bet.

Spaulding: Now, this is what I wanted to talk to you about, Mr. Chandler. How would you like to finance a scientific expedition?
Chandler: Well, that's a question.

Spaulding: I congratulate you, Mr. Chandler. And that brings us right back to where we were.

Spaulding: Yes, that *is* a question. You certainly know a question when you see it.

Spaulding: How would you like to finance a scientific expedition?
Chandler: Well is there any particular kind of expedition you have in mind?

Spaulding: Well, I'll tell you. I'm getting along in years now, and there's one thing that I always wanted to do before I quit.
Chandler: What is that?

Spaulding: Retire.

Spaulding: Now would you be interested in a proposition of that kind?

Spaulding: You know, I've always had an idea that my retirement would be the greatest contribution to Science that the world has ever known. This is your chance, Mr. Chandler. When I think what you've done for this country . . . and by the way, what have you done for this country?

Chandler: Oh, well, I've always tried to do what I could . . . especially in the world of art.

Spaulding: Art! Well, I don't know how we drifted around to it, but what is your opinion of art?

Chandler: I'm very glad you asked me . . . I . . .

Spaulding: I withdraw the question.

Spaulding: This fellow takes things seriously. It isn't safe to ask him a simple question.

Spaulding: Tell me, Mr. Chandler, where are you planning on putting your new Opera house?
Chandler: Oh, I thought I should like to put it somewhere near Central Park.

Spaulding: I *see*, why don't you put it right in Central Park?
Chandler: Could we do that?

Spaulding: Sure, do it at night when no one is looking.

Spaulding: Why not put it in the reservoir and get the whole thing over with. Of course, that might interfere with the water supply. But, after all, we must remember that art is art.

Spaulding: Still on the other hand, water is water, isn't it? And East is East, and West is West.

Spaulding: And if you take cranberries and stew them like applesauce they taste much more like prunes than rhubarb does.

Spaulding: Now you tell me what you know.

Chandler: Well, I . . . I would be very glad to give you my opinions.

Spaulding: Well, that's dandy. I'll ask you for them someday. Remind me, will you?

Spaulding: I'll tell you what, can you come to my office at ten o'clock tomorrow morning? If I'm not there, ask for Mr. Jamison, that's my secretary, and if he sees you, I'll discharge him.

Spaulding: That's a date now. Saturday at three. No, you'd better make it Tuesday. I'm going to Europe Monday.

Spaulding: Pardon me, my name's Spaulding, I've always wanted to meet you, Mr. Chandler.

Spaulding: Tell me what do you think of the traffic problem?

Spaulding: What do you think of the marriage problem?

Spaulding: What do you think of at night when you go to bed?

Spaulding: You beast!

Chandler: Well, I'll tell you, my dear . . .

Spaulding: I'd rather not discuss it any further.

Chandler: Well, you see my dear Captain, in the last analysis, it is a question of money. You see, the nickel today is not what it used to be ten years ago.

Spaulding: Remember there are children present.

Spaulding: Well, I'll go further than that. I'll get off at the depot. The nickel today is not what it was fifteen years ago. Do you know what this country needs today?

Chandler: What?
Spaulding: A seven cent nickel.

Spaulding: Yes siree, we've been using the five-cent nickel in this country since 1492. Now that's pretty near 100 years daylight saving.

Spaulding: Now why not give the seven cent nickel a chance? If that works out, next year we can have an eight cent nickel. Think what that would mean?

Spaulding: You could go to a newsstand, buy a three cent newspaper, and get the same nickel back again.

Spaulding: One nickel carefully used would last a family a life-time.

Chandler: Captain Spaulding, I think that is a wonderful idea.
Spaulding: You do, eh?
Chandler: Yes.

Spaulding: Well, then there can't be much to it. Forget about it.

Chandler: Well, well, tell me, Captain Chandler, er — excuse me, . . . Spaulding.

Spaulding: Yes, Spaulding, that's right. I'm Spaulding and you're Chandler.

Spaulding: Let's have no more of that either. Bad enough being Spaulding.

Chandler: Well, tell me Captain Spaulding...

Chandler: Spaulding is the name.
Spaulding: That's right . . . that's right. I'm Ch---- I'm Spaulding.

Spaulding: Could I look at a program a minute. I might be the news weekly for all he knows, or coming next week.

Chandler: Well, tell me, Captain Spaulding, you've been quite a traveller. What do you think about South America. I'm going there very soon, you know.

Spaulding: Is that so, where are you going?
Chandler: Uruguay.

Spaulding: Well, you go Uruguay and I'll go mine.

Spaulding: Say, how long has this been going on? Let's change the subject.

Spaulding: Take the foreign situation, take Abyssinia.

Spaulding: I'll tell you, you take Abyssinia and I'll take a hot butterscotch sundae on rye bread.

Spaulding: Let's go and see what the boys in the back room will have.

A matter of ethics.

Fancy footwork.

Mrs. Rittenhouse: I want to speak to you about the music.

Mrs. Rittenhouse: What's the matter with you?

Mrs. Rittenhouse: I think it would be nice . . .

Mrs. Rittenhouse: Good gracious!

Mrs. Rittenhouse: Well, well, what's this?

Mrs. Rittenhouse: Oh my dear . . . I don't know what . . .

Mrs. Whitehead: Hello Professor!

Mrs. Whitehead: Good heavens!

Mrs. Whitehead: What's the matter with his feet?

Mrs. Whitehead: Oh!...
Have you ever...This is embarrassing!
Ravelli: Ha, ha, ha!

Ravelli: Oh, it's nothing, you see. Why we play all kinds of games...we play blackjack...

Ravelli: Soccer . . .

Ravelli: Ah! What's the
matter for you?
Mrs. Rittenhouse: Oh, Oh!

Mrs. Rittenhouse: Mrs. Whitehead, I'm . . .

Mrs. Whitehead: Get your foot off . . .

Mrs. Whitehead: For heaven's sake . . .

Mrs. Whitehead: What's the matter . . .

Mrs. Rittenhouse: I wouldn't have had this happen for the world. Oh, good heavens!

Mrs. Rittenhouse: Why, this is terrible!

Mrs. Rittenhouse: Let go of me!

Mrs. Rittenhouse: Let go of me!

Ravelli: 1----

Ravelli: 2----

Ravelli: 3----

Ravelli: Thata boy!

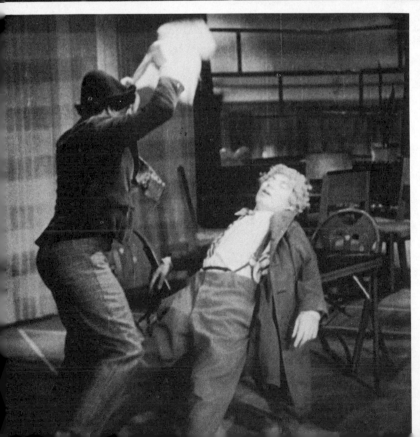

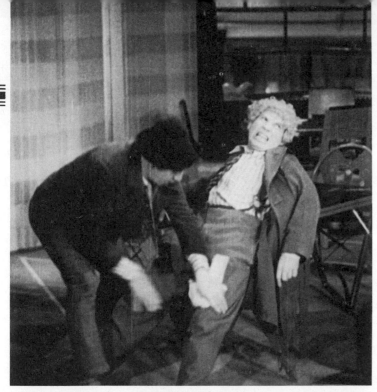
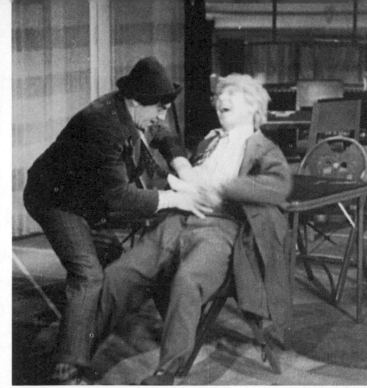
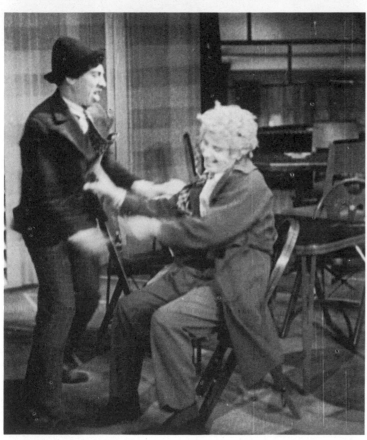

Mrs. Rittenhouse: Good heavens! Oh dear! . . . I must get them out of here. What can I do?

Mrs. Whitehead: I don't know. You better get Hives.

Mrs. Rittenhouse: No, no, let me get him. I'm just trying to watch my chance to slip out, and get Hives... Oh, this is terrible!

Mrs. Whitehead: It's disgraceful!

Mrs. Rittenhouse: Oh! Go away from me.

Ravelli: She can't take it there!

Mrs. Rittenhouse: Oh!

Mrs. Rittenhouse: Oh!

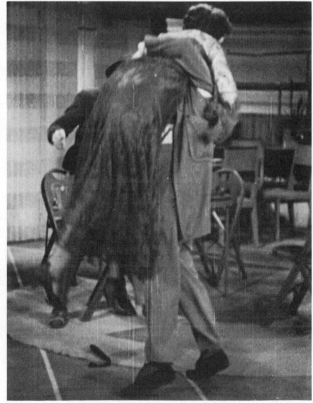

Mrs. Rittenhouse: Oh!

Mrs. Rittenhouse: Get away from me.

Mrs. Rittenhouse: Oh, it's disgraceful!
Ravelli: Well, why don't you leave him alone?

The art of
communicating
with
The Professor.

Hey, quiet! . . . quiet!

146

That's the flash.

The African Lecture

Mrs. Rittenhouse: And now, my friends, before we start the musical program, Captain Spaulding has kindly consented to tell us about his trip to Africa.

Mrs. Rittenhouse: Captain Spaulding . . .
Spaulding: Me?

Spaulding: My friends, I am going to tell you of that great, mysterious, wonderful continent known as Africa.

Spaulding: Africa is God's country and he can have it.

Spaulding: Well, sir, we left N.Y. drunk and early on the morning of February second. After fifteen days on the water and six on the boat, we finally arrived on the shores of Africa.

Spaulding: We at once proceeded three hundred miles into the heart of the jungle where I shot a polar bear.

Spaulding: This bear was six feet seven inches in his stocking feet and had shoes on.

Mrs. Rittenhouse: Pardon me just a moment, Captain, just a moment. I always thought polar bears lived in the frozen north.

Spaulding: Oh, you did?

Spaulding: Well, this bear was anemic, and he couldn't stand the cold climate.

Spaulding: He was a rich bear and he could afford to go away in the winter.

Spaulding: You take care of your animals and I'll take care of mine.

Spaulding: Frozen north, my eye.

Spaulding: From the day of our arrival
we led an active life.

Spaulding: The first morning saw us up
at six, breakfasted and back in bed at seven.

Spaulding: This was our routine for the first three months. We finally got so we were back in bed by six-thirty.

Spaulding: One morning I was sitting in front of the cabin smoking some meat... when...

Mrs. Rittenhouse: Smoking some meat...?

Spaulding: Yes, there wasn't a cigar store in the neighborhood.

Spaulding: As I say, I was sitting in front of the cabin when I bagged six tigers... This was the biggest lot...

Mrs. Rittenhouse: Oh, Captain, Captain, did you catch six tigers?

Spaulding: I bagged them... I bagged them to go away...

Spaulding: But they hung around all afternoon.

Spaulding: They were the most persistent tigers I have ever seen.

Spaulding: The principal animals inhabiting the African jungle are moose, elks, and Knights of Pythias.

Spaulding: Of course, you all know what a moose is. That's big game.

Spaulding: The first day I shot two bucks. That was the biggest game we had.

Spaulding: As I say, you all know what a moose is. A moose runs around the floor, eats cheese and is chased by the cats.

Spaulding: The elks, on the other hand, live up in the hills and in the spring they come down for their annual convention.

Spaulding: It is very interesting to watch them come down to the water hole. And you should see them run when they find that it's only a water hole.

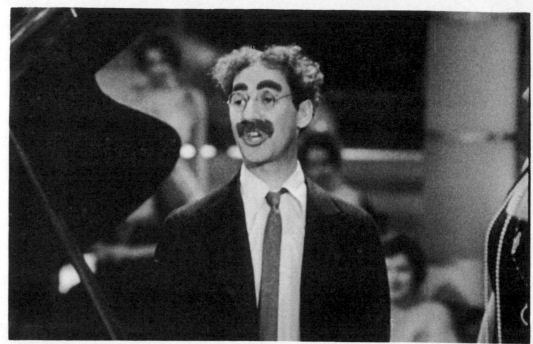

Spaulding: What they are looking for is an elcohol.
One morning I shot an elephant in my pajamas. How he
got in my pajamas, I don't know.

Spaulding: Then we tried to remove the tusks. The tusks.

Spaulding: That's not so easy to say. Tusks. You try it some time.

Chandler: Oh, simple. Tusks.

Spaulding: Pardon me, my name is Spaulding. I've always wanted to meet you, Mr. Chandler.

Spaulding: As I say, we tried to remove the tusks.

Spaulding: But they were embedded so firmly we couldn't budge them.

Spaulding: Of course, in Alabama, the Tuscaloosa

Spaulding: but that is entirely ir-elephant to what I was talking about.

Spaulding: We took some pictures of the native girls, but they weren't developed.

Spaulding: But we're going back again in a couple of weeks. Now . . .

Mrs. Rittenhouse: A very enlightening speech, Captain.

Chandler: Three cheers for Captain Spaulding! Three cheers for Captain Spaulding!

Chandler: Three cheers for Captain Spaulding!

Chandler: Three cheers—

Mrs. Rittenhouse: No one asked for chairs. Put them right where you found them. Go, go on. Go on, get out.

Chandler: Go on, go on, you.

Mrs. Rittenhouse: And now, friends, Signor Ravelli will oblige us at the piano.

Mrs. Rittenhouse: Signor Ravelli.

Spaulding: Signor Ravelli's first selection will be "Somewhere My Love Lies Sleeping" with a male chorus.

Spaulding: And now, Mrs. Rittenrotten, I have a surprise for you.
Mrs. Rittenhouse: Mrs. Rittenhouse!
Spaulding: Yes. Slight error. I've a little surprise for you. The man is here for the piano.
Mrs. Rittenhouse: Oh, Captain . . .

Spaulding: No, really, what I mean to say is, when I departed from the natives of Africa, I was presented with a little gift, and this gift, I'm going to give to you at a very low figure.
Mrs. Rittenhouse: Oh, how wonderful, Captain.

Spaulding: This is all hand painted. The whole thing was done with the white of an egg.
Mrs. Rittenhouse: What is it Captain, what *is* it?

Spaulding: What is it you ask. It's a hope chest for a guinea pig.

Spaulding: Oh, what is it! Now, this magnificent chest,

Spaulding: No, this,

Spaulding: No, this magnificent chest I now take pleasure in presenting to you with my compliments.

Mrs. Rittenhouse: Captain, this leaves me speechless.

Spaulding: Well, see that you remain that way.

Though a masterpiece has been stolen, Spaulding's main concern is his bruised ego.

Though a masterpiece has been stolen, Spaulding's main concern is his bruised ego.

Spaulding: Dear Elsie, no, never mind Elsie.
Jamison: Do you want me to scratch Elsie?
Spaulding: Well, if you enjoy that sort of thing, it's quite alright with me. However, I'm not interested in your private affairs, Jamison. Begin this way . . . let's start all over again . . .
Note: The above dialogue was cut from the film, but appears in the script continuity.

Jamison: Dear Elsie, scratch.
Spaulding: That won't do, Jamison. That won't go thru the mail the way you've got the letter. The way you've got it, McCormick is scratching Elsie. You had better turn that around and have Elsie scratch McCormick. You'd better turn McCormick around too, Jamison and see what you can do for me.

Note: The above dialogue was cut from the film, but appears in the script continuity.

Hennessey: Mrs. Rittenhouse?
Mrs. Rittenhouse: Yes.
Hennessey: I'm Inspector Hennessey from headquarters.
Mrs. Rittenhouse: How do you do?

Spaulding: Let me introduce myself.

Spaulding: I'm Captain Scotland of Spaulding Yard. No . . . Captain Spaulding of Scotland Yard. Please don't make the same mistake again.
Hennessey: I'm glad to know you, Captain.

Spaulding: Well, I should think you would be. Now then, Inspector.

Spaulding: I think between the two of us, we can solve the mystery of the stolen painting. Especially if you go home.

Mrs. Rittenhouse: Inspector, please don't be too hasty about making an arrest. I don't want any of my guests embarrassed.

Hennessey: Don't worry. We won't arrest anybody.

Spaulding: He's lucky if he can stay out of jail himself.

Mrs. Rittenhouse: Mr. Jamison, would you mind taking the Inspector and his men to the Library and showing them the scene of the crime?

Jamison: Certainly, Mrs. Rittenhouse. Right this way, Inspector.
Hennessey: Come on, boys.

Spaulding: And, Jamison . . . count the spoons.

Mrs. Rittenhouse: Oh, Captain, I didn't know you had been a detective too.
Spaulding: There's a whole lot of things you don't know.
Mrs. Rittenhouse: I suppose that's so.

Spaulding: You know darn well it's so. Where were you on the night of June 5, 1774?
Mrs. Rittenhouse: I'm afraid I don't know.

Spaulding: You bet you don't know. Where was I?
Mrs. Rittenhouse: I don't know.
Spaulding: Well, I don't know either.

Spaulding: And if I did, I wouldn't tell you. Put that in your pipe and smoke it.

Spaulding: Take a number from one to ten.
Mrs. Rittenhouse: Alright.
Spaulding: Alright, what's the number?
Mrs. Rittenhouse: Seven.
Spaulding: That's right. Seven is right.

Spaulding: I could have done it with one hand if I wanted to. This is no mystery, I could solve this in five minutes if I wanted to worry.

Mrs. Rittenhouse: Captain, I don't want you to worry. I don't want anything to interfere with your week-end.

Spaulding: Nothing ever interferes with my weakend and I'll thank you not to get personal, Mrs. Rittenhouse.
Mrs. Rittenhouse: Oh, Captain.

Spaulding: Where's my secretary?
Mrs. Rittenhouse: But I assure you, I didn't mean to offend you.
Spaulding: No . . . no . . . no . . . where's my secretary . . . Jamison . . . Jamison . . .

Mrs. Rittenhouse: Oh, please, Captain, you misunderstand me . . . I didn't mean it that way . . .
Spaulding: A more dastardly crack I've never heard.

Mrs. Rittenhouse: Oh, Captain . . .
Spaulding: I wish I were back in the jungle where men are monkeys.

Mrs. Rittenhouse: Captain, I'm so sorry.
Spaulding: Jamison . . . Jamison . . . JAMISON!

Mrs. Rittenhouse: Oh, Captain! Oh, dear!

The art of communicating with Ravelli.

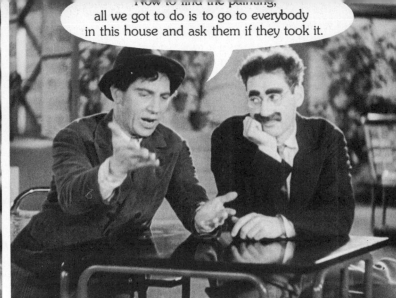

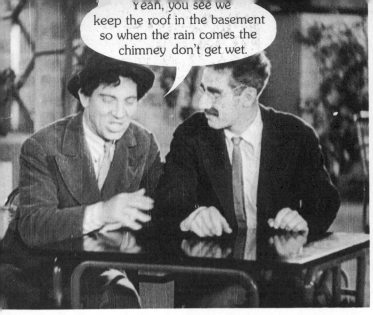

Something's up The Professor's sleeve!

Hennessey:
You'd better come with me, young fellow.

Spaulding:
Don't take him away officer. He returned the painting.

Spaulding:
Pardon me, my name is Spaulding. I always wanted to meet you.

Hennessey: Alright, I'll let him go this time, but I want to give you some advice.

Hennessey: You're running around with the wrong kind of people.

Hennessey: Do you want to be a crook?

Hennessey: Why don't you go home?

Ravelli: He's got no home.
Hennessey: Go home for a few nights and stay home. Don't you know

Hennessey: your poor old mother sits there night after...

CLONK!

218

Hennessey: night after night waiting to hear your step on the stairs.
Ravelli: Got no stairs.
Hennessey: And I can see a little light burning in . . . burning in the window . . .

Spaulding: No, you can't. The gas company turned it off.

CLONK!

Hennessey: Now what I'm telling you is for your own good, and if you'll listen to me you can't go wrong.

Spaulding: This may go on for years.

Hennessey: Now there's just one thing...

Spaulding: I can't understand what's delaying that coffee pot?

Spaulding: Where's the cream?

Hennessy: Well, you certainly surprise me.

Spaulding: Me, too. I thought he had more than that.